Published by Rock N' Roll Colouring Ltd® 2024

© 2024 Megadeth Under License to Manhead LLC.
Produced by Rock N' Roll Colouring Ltd

Designer: Mark Leary at Asylumseventy7

All rights reserved. No portion of this book may be reproduced, stored in a retrieval system, or transmitted in any form or by any means, mechanical, electronic, photocopying, recording, or otherwise, without permission from the publisher.

First published in the UK by Rock N' Roll Colouring Ltd®
London
www.rocknrollcolouring.com

ISBN: 9781838147037

Printed in the UK by W&G Baird

The Official Megadeth Colouring Book

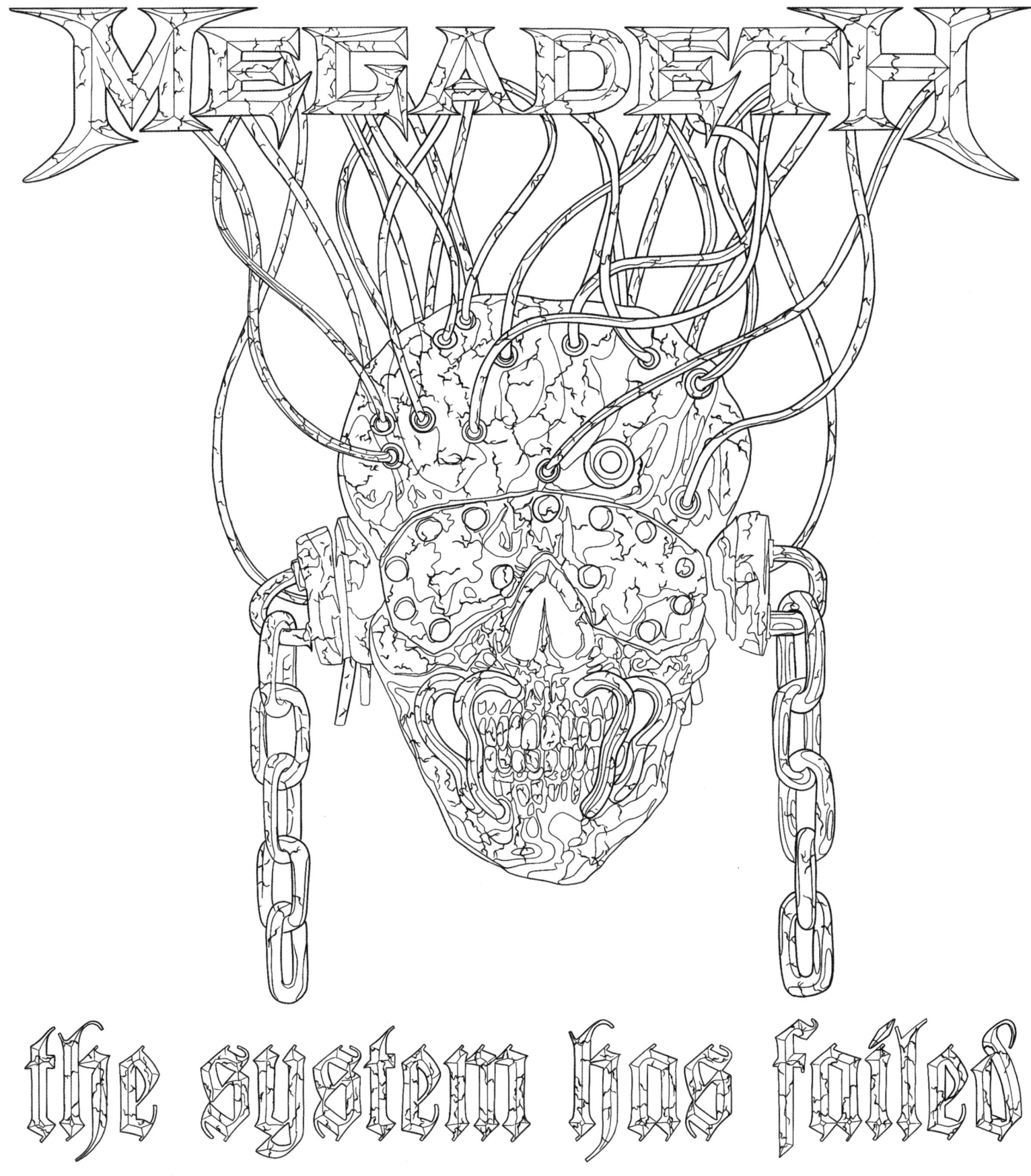

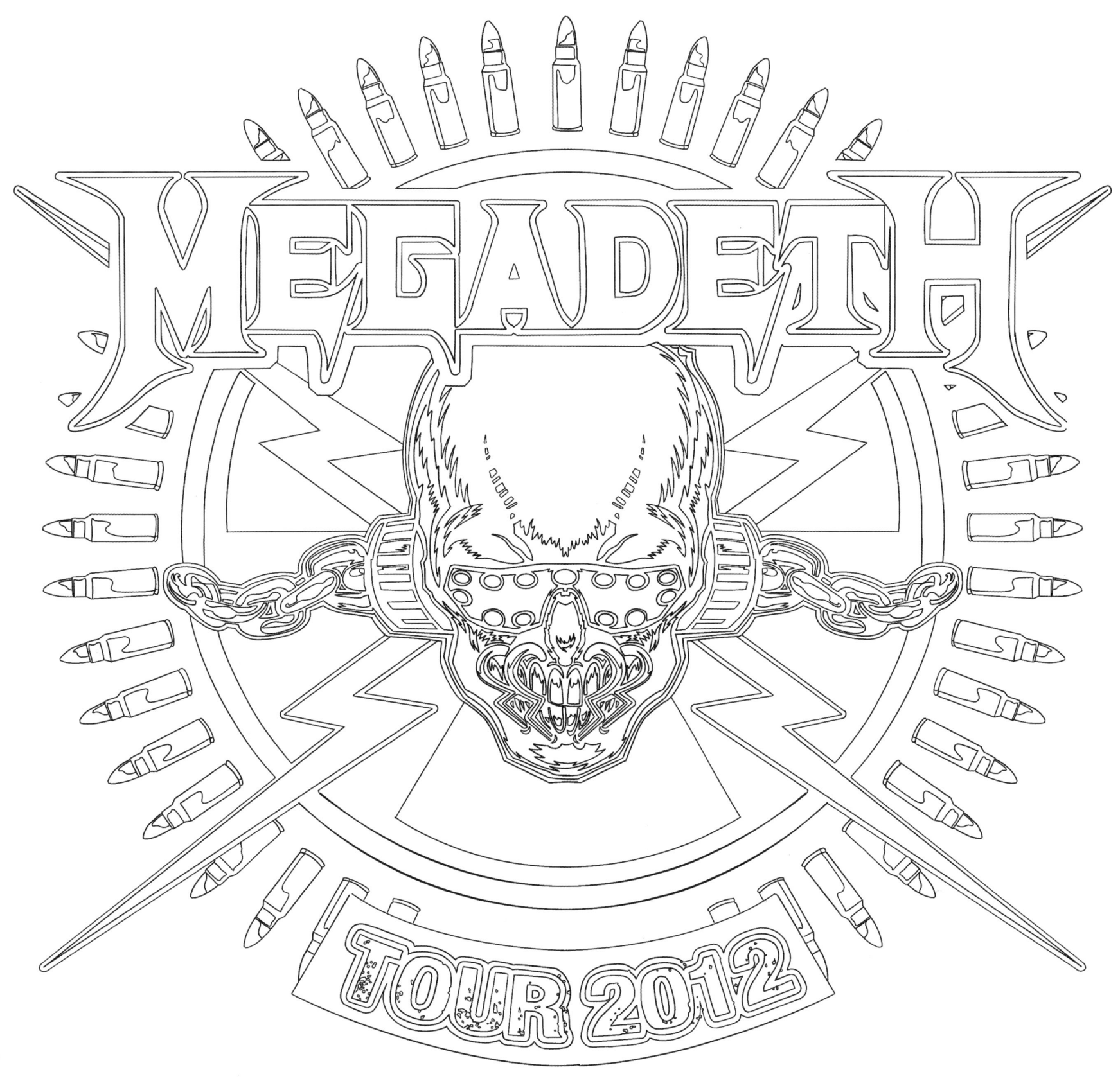

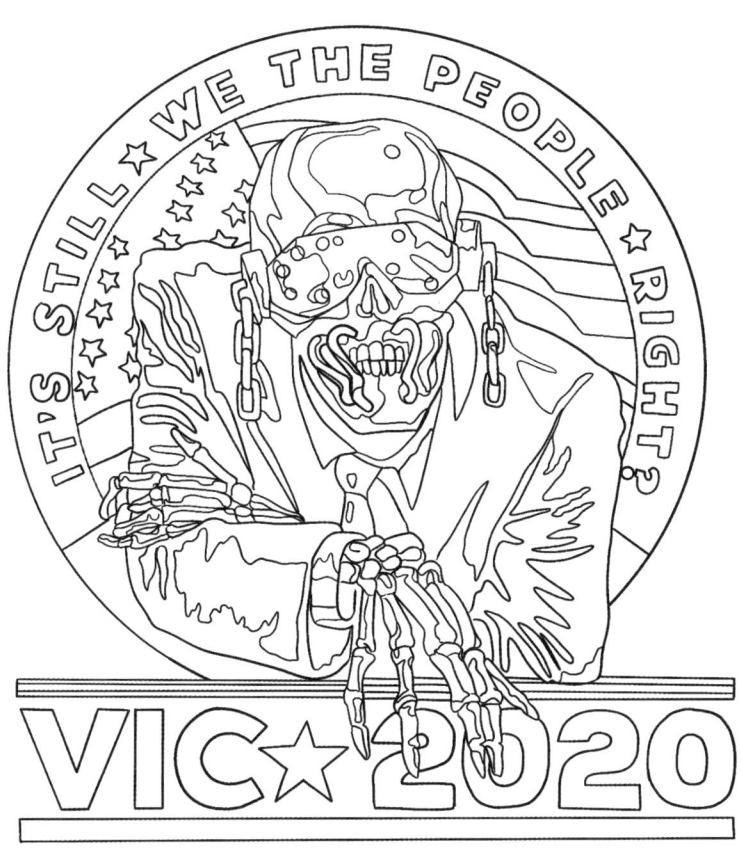

For your doodles